Introduction

You've studied the newspaper advertisements and compared specifications. You've decided on a bundle deal which suits your needs and finances. You've pinned a salesperson down on a really good deal and handed over your credit card or, maybe, used the net at a friend's place and ordered one from a computer vendor's website. The moment has arrived.

The boxes are sitting on the floor in front of you – mission accomplished. The hard work's done, right? Sorry to be the one to break it to you, but the fun and games start here.

So, before you break out the paper knife and slit all those boxes open... STOP! It's worth spending a few minutes considering the space, the light, and how the computer's going to be set up, before you start taking bits out and assembling them. Take a good hard look at the place you intend to set your computer up, the desk, the chair you plan to use, the nearest window and/or light source. Make sure you know what's in which box so you can assemble your system methodically and not end up losing the driver disks or wondering which piece this cable is for. Sit down with a cup of tea and the instruction leaflets to understand the way your particular computer should be set up.

If necessary, refer to the extensive glossary at the back of this book. When you find an unfamiliar word in this book, if it's in **bold** type, there's more information in the glossary.

THANK YOU

My grateful thanks are due to many people for their help in preparing this volume. In particular I acknowledge with gratitude the generous access to the Mac brains of Bill, Tony, Garry, Geoff, Julian, Kathie and Peter, and to Paul for opening the Window on XP.

As you flick through this book you'll find boxes, just like this, at the start of each chapter. They'll tell you what material you'll find on the CD-ROM at the back of the book pertaining to that chapter.

HELEN DANCER

Contents

Your workspace

Since you've just spent a substantial amount of money on your computer, it's important that you are as comfortable as possible using it. This means giving some thought to where it's going to live, the natural and other available light and, significantly, the desk and chair you're going to use.

Light

It's important to consider the light, both for daytime and nighttime use of the computer. A natural light source can be a blessing and a curse; strong sunlight from behind can cause an intolerable amount of screen glare. An ideal set-up is a room with a skylight – so that the natural light comes from above – but if that's not possible, position your desk so that any natural light comes from either one side or the other, and supplement this with good overhead light from a desk lamp or fitted ceiling light. Avoid light shining onto your **monitor** – the reflection will quickly tire your eyes and you'll start to squint, and this will, in time, promote headaches.

Desk

There are a wide range of specially designed computer "workstations" – a fancy name for a piece of furniture that crosses over between desk, shelf and cupboard – available at reasonable prices, and you might decide that, if space is at a premium at your place, a workstation is a good idea. If that's your plan, spend some time sitting at them at the shop. Work out if you're really comfortable and could sit there for an hour or more at a time, and whether they have as many nooks and crannies as you'll need. Is there a place to put the speakers? What about the printer and **scanner**, and the paper they use? Is there enough space at the side for any books or other material you may need to work from?

CHOOSING THE RIGHT ROOM

You will already have thought about the room in which your computer's going to live, and hopefully you have a quiet corner set aside. There's no fun in trying to concentrate on a project with a TV blaring in the background, or lots of passing foot traffic. Alternatively, if one of the prime reasons for having a computer is to help with the children's education, and that computer is to be connected to the **internet**, then having it in a common space is quite important, so that you can monitor what they are doing and help them learn safe and responsible **surfing**.

On the CD-ROM:
- Gentle stretching exercises
- How to prevent eyestrain

POWER SURGE PROTECTOR/UPS

Installing a **UPS**, or Uninterruptible Power Supply box, can be a lifesaver if the area you live in suffers from frequent power surges or is prone to blackouts. A UPS kicks in when it senses either a surge or a loss of mains power, and will provide you with those precious extra few minutes to save your work before the computer blacks out, or ensure a nice even current stream if it senses a power surge, which might otherwise damage the delicate circuitry inside your computer.

If there is not enough room for all of your computer's extra bits, will you have another desk close by for the **peripherals** and stationery? Will the cables be long enough to reach between your **system unit** and other devices that need to plug into it? Is the desk deep enough to accommodate the size of the **monitor** you've chosen? Can air flow behind the system unit and monitor, to stop them from overheating?

You'll need to ensure that the desk you choose is deep enough for the monitor, not only so that air can flow behind the system unit and the monitor, but also so that you're not sitting with your nose pressed against the screen. Your monitor should be at least at arm's length from where you're sitting, and at eye level, so you're not slouching or craning.

If you have a computer with a desktop system unit, sitting the monitor on top of it should make it a comfortable height. If you have a tower case – which sits next to the monitor or on the floor – and you are using a standard desk or table and feel that your monitor is too low, the most cost-effective solution is to put it on top of an old telephone directory.

The desk you choose can make all the difference between an organised and comfortable computing experience, and a mildly (or even intensely) chaotic and frustrated one.

Chair

If you plan to place your monitor on an existing table in your house, the most important consideration is the relationship between the height of the desk and the height of the chair.

You should be sitting comfortably so that the top of your monitor is at eye level and your keyboard is neither too high nor too low. Your elbows should be able to rest on the arms of the chair or on the desk between you and the keyboard, to minimise neck and shoulder strain from prolonged typing.

An office chair with a contoured back and gas lift, even arms, is probably just as good an investment (if not more so) as a workstation – you can get away with a standard desk or table if you can adjust your chair and get comfortable.

A bad chair or, let's face it, a chair that was designed with dinner in mind, rather than hours in front of a computer, will contribute to you feeling tired and uncomfortable.

Keyboard

The keyboard should not be jammed right up under the monitor, or right under your nose. Find a position on the desk for your keyboard so you don't have to stretch your arms to reach it, or cramp your elbows to type. Either of these options will become tiring very quickly and promote neck ache and, in the long term, can contribute to RSI (Repetitive Strain Injury). There are various ergonomic wrist-rest products available, which claim to support your forearms while typing, if you find that, even with the perfect chair/desk height ratio, you are experiencing arm fatigue. Alternatively, most standard desktop keyboards have little legs that flip out to slightly raise the top of the keyboard, which may prove a more comfortable solution.

Cables

Most cables are cut at a length that assumes all the pieces of your system are going to sit reasonably close to each other – and extra lengths of cable behind the machine are messy and annoying. But if you have another office set-up in mind and need extra-long cables to join, say, your computer to your printer (because they will sit on separate desks), specify the length you need up front, rather than get home and realise you need to swap the cable or, worse still, buy another one.

Be careful to avoid tangling the various cables that join the parts of your system to the system unit, and make sure that both the mouse and keyboard cords can be extended freely.

It's also important to ensure that the whole system is close to a power source and that there are enough power plugs to accommodate all the devices without overloading one power point or power board. Avoid running a power cord across a room or hallway to plug in your computer; this is unsightly as well as unsafe. Likewise, if you plan to connect your computer to the **internet**, there should be a telephone outlet for your **modem** nearby. It's well worth considering installing an extension, or even a second line close to where your computer is going to live, to avoid stringing metres of phone line between the computer and the telephone point.

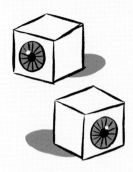

EYE STRAIN

You can minimise the potential physical strain of sitting for long periods at a computer if the light is good, and if the height of the chair/desk and support for your elbows means you are comfortable and relaxed. It's a good idea, however, to remember to take regular screen breaks for the sake of your eyes. It's as simple as taking a few minutes every half hour to look out a window and focus on something in the middle distance, stare at it for a minute, and then look straight back at the screen. You won't feel any difference, but your eyes will have had some valuable shifting focus exercise.

What's in the boxes?

Checklist

For a standard PC
(Intel/Windows machine)

In the main box you should find the **system unit**. On the front of the system unit you should see:

- a floppy disk slot
- a closed **CD-ROM** or **DVD** drive. CD-ROM and DVD drives are retractable, and pushing a button will make them slide out and back in. Don't try and pull the CD-ROM drive out, or push it back in manually. These drives won't work until the power is turned on.

The main box should also contain the following:

- a power cord
- a mouse
- a keyboard
- an instruction booklet
- a warranty card
- operating system discs (i.e., Windows) and any applications software CDs, even if they have already been installed, including anti-virus software.

In the **monitor** box, you should find:

- a monitor (screen)
- connector cable to plug into the system unit
- a power cable
- an instruction booklet
- a warranty card.

For an Apple iMac

The boxes should contain an all-in one **system unit**, speakers and screen, as well as the following:

- a keyboard
- a mouse
- a power cord
- a **Firewire** camera cable
- iMovie 2 software
- an instruction booklet
- a warranty card
- operating system discs for Mac OS 9 and Mac OS X and any applications software CDs, even if they have already been installed.

For an Apple G4

The boxes should contain an Apple G4 **system unit** (the **monitor** and system unit will be in different boxes), as well as the following:

- a keyboard
- a mouse
- hardware-testing software
- a power cable
- iMovie 2 software
- an instruction booklet
- a warranty card
- operating system discs for Mac OS 9 and Mac OS X and any applications software CDs, even if they have already been installed.

The **LCD** monitor for the G4 needs no separate power cable, but plugs into the system unit and takes its power from there. A third party monitor will, however, require its own power source.

The printer

The box containing the printer should also come with the following:

- a power cord
- a connecting cable (parallel or **USB**)
- a driver CD
- ink cartridges
- an instruction booklet
- a warranty card.

The modem

If you've chosen an external **modem**, the box should contain the following:

- a modem
- a connector cable
- a power cord
- a telephone line cable
- a driver CD
- an instruction booklet
- a warranty card.

The speakers

The speaker box should contain the following:

- two speakers
- an instruction booklet
- a warranty card
- a power cord.

The digital camera

If you've chosen a **digital camera**, the box should contain the following:

- a digital camera
- a connecting cable (serial, USB or Firewire)
- an audio/video cable (if your camera can record sound and video)
- batteries (rechargeable batteries are probably a good investment in the long run)
- a Flash card (a RAM card on which you can store extra images)
- an instruction booklet
- a warranty card.

The scanner

The **scanner** box should include the following:

- a scanner
- a connecting cable (serial or USB)
- a power cord
- a driver CD
- an instruction booklet
- a warranty card.

Connecting your computer

Computer companies are finally getting on the bandwagon to make this process as simple as possible; most offer diagrams in the box, and many even have colour-coded cables and points, making the task completely foolproof.

Since most computers have **peripherals**, each with their own power cables, the most practical way of setting up is to buy a good quality power board to plug all your various components into, rather than putting different plugs in different sockets, and running leads all over the place. Be careful not to overload the power board, and don't be tempted to put a double adaptor in it to accommodate just one more plug. Thinking through your power requirements *before* you start is going to make your job a lot easier.

Place the power pack behind the **system unit**. Sit the system unit on the desk or the floor, depending on whether it is a tower or desktop case, and the **monitor** on the desk. Plug the monitor cable into the monitor then the system unit, following the diagram on the next page.

CORDS AND LEADS

Most standard phone or **modem** cords are about two metres long, and you should avoid having to stretch them across floors or hallways between the outlet and the computer. If the distance from the phone line to the computer is greater, extension leads can be purchased from electronics shops or phone retailers. It's important, however, to take care to tape the cord down between the outlet and computer, as a household safety precaution.

On the CD-ROM:
■ Contact and website information for your chosen supplier
■ Applications for your handheld computer
■ Monitoring/filtering software

Connecting an iMac
rough guide only – will depend on model

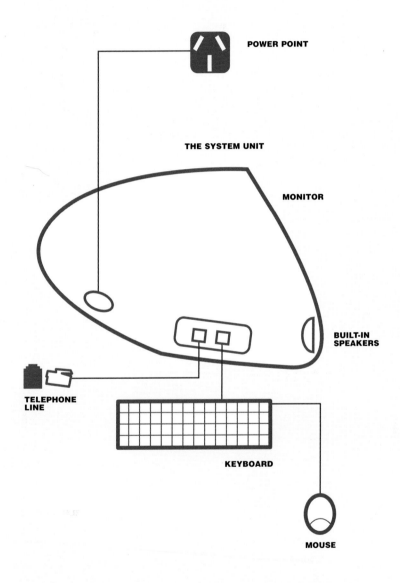

POWER POINT

THE SYSTEM UNIT

MONITOR

BUILT-IN SPEAKERS

TELEPHONE LINE

KEYBOARD

MOUSE

Connecting a PC
rough guide only – will depend on model

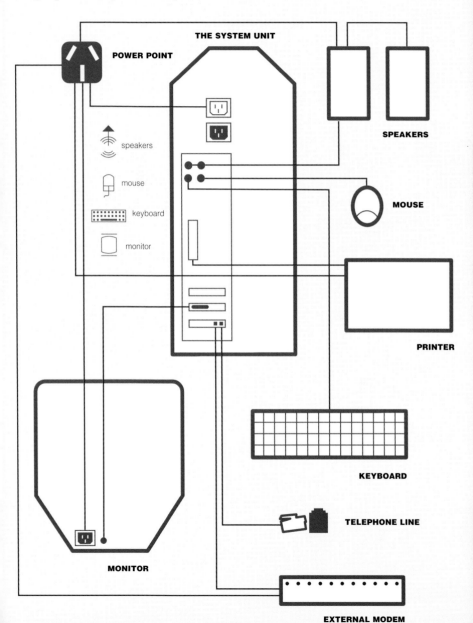

THE SYSTEM UNIT

POWER POINT

speakers

mouse

keyboard

monitor

SPEAKERS

MOUSE

PRINTER

KEYBOARD

TELEPHONE LINE

MONITOR

EXTERNAL MODEM

If you've bought an iMac, the job is a lot easier, because the **monitor** and **system unit** are rolled into one box.

Plug the mouse into the back of the system unit (on the side if it's an iMac), then the keyboard. Make sure you can extend your mouse cord freely and that it's not tangled. Decide whether you're going to use the mouse with your right or left hand, and set the mouse on the mousepad on the side of the keyboard you prefer. If you have external speakers, check which one has the on/off button, and plug that one into the appropriate jack. Plug the second speaker's lead into the first speaker, and arrange them so your sound is even.

Take the printer (or any **peripherals** you have to add on) out of its box, and attach it to the computer, and then plug it into the power board.

If you have an internal **modem**, attach the cable that looks like a phone lead to the back of the computer, then into the telephone socket. If you have an external modem, sit the modem adjacent to the system unit and plug the connector cable into the computer, then plug the power cord into the power source and one end of the telephone lead into the back of the modem where it says "Line"; the other end goes into the telephone socket in the wall.

Sit down at the desk and make sure everything is within reach and, if it is, switch your power source on at the wall and press the "on" button on the computer.

Connecting other peripherals

The process for connecting other peripherals, such as a **digital camera**, CD writer, back-up drive or a **scanner** is quite standard, irrespective of what kind of device it is.

Firstly, plug the new device in. The advent of Plug and Play, a standard specification for making peripheral devices talk to the host computer, means there's no need to turn the computer off to do this. However, some manufacturers' instructions specifically ask you not to plug it in while the computer's running, so check the instructions that come with the device. If your computer is a hand-me-down, however, and is more than three years old, it's advisable to plug your new toy in before you boot your computer up.

For a standard PC

Next, make sure that all other applications are shut down. This means the computer doesn't have to work so hard at finding **files** and **drivers**, because it only has to concentrate on that one task – this way, if something goes wrong with installation and you have to reboot the computer, you won't lose any unsaved work.

Windows XP has more than 12,000 drivers pre-installed, so chances are that one of them will match your device, and you won't have to do anything. When you plug in your printer or camera, the computer will search its memory banks, find the compatible driver and load it automatically. On the rare occasion you'll need to use the drivers that come in the printer box, simply choose Have Disk as you step through the installation process, which you'll find in

Control Panel. This installation process will run automatically, and tell you when it is finished, and you can simply start using the device straightaway.

HELP!

Today's computers are a far cry from the recalcitrant boxes we used to bring home, string up, and struggle with. Setting up a home computer today really is completely simple. The vendor will pre-install the operating and applications software for you, and it will work perfectly well right out of the box. However, if the thought of connecting your computer still seems daunting, there's help at hand – but it will cost.

Either the manufacturer (if you buy direct), the reseller or the retailer can arrange for someone to come to your house and set up your computer, but expect that it will add a couple of hundred dollars to your purchase price.

So think of what you could do with that money instead, be bold and give it a go. The feeling of having accomplished it all by yourself is only moments away!

For an Apple iMac

Adding new **hardware** to your Macintosh is so simple it hardly needs to be written about. Because of new connection technologies and standards, such as **USB** and **Firewire**, that Mac has made mandatory for the connections and cables between Macs and **peripherals**, they can be "hot-plugged", which means they won't suffer from being plugged in while the computer's active. When you plug the new device in, your iMac will recognise that something has changed, look at the new device and ask the user, "So, you want to add this video camera?" (or whatever the device is). All you need do is click on OK, and it's done. For a device, such as a printer, which requires the manufacturer's own software **drivers**, simply go to the Apple menu (running Mac OS 9), select Chooser and follow the instructions to add the software drivers, then select that new printer as the default printer for your machine. If you are running Mac OS X use the Print Centre application in the Applications folder.

Synching a handheld computer to your desktop

A **handheld computer** can be a boon, enabling you to take information from your computer and carry it around.

"Synching", or synchronising, your handheld computer to your **desktop** is the process of transferring the information that's new in one, to the other, so that both feed each other and are equally up-to-date. For example, if you want to create a list of names and addresses, it's faster and easier to use your desktop keyboard than the tiny keyboard or graffiti script that handhelds use to enter data. Transferring that list to your handheld means you can take it with you and have access to the information wherever you go. While you're out, if you run into a friend who has recently moved, you can update the details in your handheld. Then, back at home, synching your handheld with your desktop will automatically update your existing address book with the new details.

Anything you add to or delete from your handheld will be updated on your desktop when you synch your handheld back in with your desktop when you come home.

Synching your handheld computer to your desktop is easy. When the computer is off, simply attach the handheld computer's cradle (also called a docking station) to your computer, using the desktop's **serial** port (COM port) or USB connection – whichever applies to your model.

Don't put the handheld in it at this stage. Turn on the computer; when it boots up, put the **software** CD in the **CD-ROM** drive and follow its on-screen instructions.

Once the software is installed, your desktop and handheld computers will recognise and talk to each other quite easily. To synchronise your data from one to the other, put the handheld in its cradle and press the button on the cradle that begins the synchronising process.

There's a wealth of software for your handheld computer; you can convert temperatures and currencies, if you're travelling, or weights and measures if you're in the kitchen. Some handheld applications are on the CD at the back of the book. To load and use them, see the inside back cover.

PHONE
NEAR-TO-HOME

Make sure that the access number for your ISP connection is a local call, especially if you live outside the metropolitan area. Phone charges apply for the use of the line, as well as the cost you'll pay to your ISP for connect time. You don't want to be paying long distance rates for your phone time if you don't have to!

Making the connection with your ISP

A quick check-list

To connect your computer to the **internet**, you'll need:

- a phone line in easy reach of your **system unit**
- a **modem** – internal or external
- an account with an **ISP** (Internet Service Provider).
- if you've decided on a faster connection, such as DSL, you should ask your ISP's technician to set up your computer when he installs the cable connection

Making the connection with Windows

When you buy a **Windows** machine with internet access as part of the bundle, you'll get an access kit on **CD-ROM**. To load up the access **software**, start as before, in Control Panel. Select Network and Internet Connections and step through the process, and when you come to the screen called Getting Ready, choose the option to "Use the CD I got from an ISP".

Making the connection with Mac

When told I was writing this chapter, a very smug Mac user remarked: "This is going to be the shortest chapter in your book. To connect an iMac to the internet, you plug the computer into the power source, plug the phone line into the phone outlet and turn it on. That's it."

Well, if you're using a modem, it's pretty much true – connecting an iMac to the internet is as simple as pie. When you first take the computer out of the box, plug it in and turn it on, it will run through a series of set up questions, part of which will be to ask you to create a log-on and password – this might be a typed-in password or a voice print, as described on page 37. Another of the standard questions is: "Do you want to connect to the internet?" Click on Yes and it will ask you for the details of the ISP you've signed up with, including the local access number.

Once you've typed that number in, that's all you have to do. The computer will first dial its home Apple Centre, and **download** any additional **drivers** it might need to work at optimum levels with the ISP and connection type nominated, and will tell you when it is finished. From there on in, making the connection with your ISP is as easy as the click of a mouse.

If you're using Mac OS 9 it will even offer to sign you up to an Apple designated ISP if you don't have an internet access kit lined up.

Direct buy

Companies such as Dell, which deals with its customers direct, over the phone or over the internet rather than through computer retailers, for example, offer a set-up and basic training package for $148, or an installation only package – i.e., take it out of the box, plug it in and switch it on – for $110. If you have bought a computer bundle which includes internet access,

and would like a technician to get your net connection up and running (probably the trickiest part of the operation), then expect to pay extra – in this case $228.

Some computer vendors also offer free phone support, included as part of the purchase price of the computer rather than as an add-on cost, for the life of the computer. Most problems are easily solved over the phone.

Computer retailer/reseller

If you buy a computer from a retailer, then you need to check whether it's the retailer or the manufacturer who will provide your service and support, and whether that service is offered in your home or RTB (Return To Base). RTB means you have to take your computer to the nearest service centre if there is anything wrong with it, and if the nearest isn't very near at all, that can prove very inconvenient. Check with your local retailer what options there are for service, should you need it.

Tips and troubleshooting

When you turn your computer on, you'll see various lights flashing. These status lights indicate that the various drives are thinking, or processing information. There's nothing untoward about that.

For example, when you put a **floppy disk** in the floppy disk drive, nothing will happen, because you haven't asked it to do anything yet, but when you try and call up a **file** from the floppy disk (more about that later), the light will come on, because it's processing, then retrieving the file. Similarly, when you put a CD in the **CD-ROM** drive and call up a file from it, the little light will blink to signify that it is processing your request.

No lights, no action

If you turn your computer on and nothing happens, the most common source of the problem has nothing to do with the system itself, but with cords and plugs not being plugged in tightly enough, or switched on. Before you start to get anxious, check all the power cables and connector cables, to make sure they are plugged in firmly to the computer and the power source, and switched on. If that's not the problem, test the power outlet in the wall with another appliance, such as a desk lamp or hair dryer. If they work, and your computer doesn't, it's probably time to call tech support.

Look ma, no picture

If you turn your computer on and it hums into life but there's nothing on the screen, again, the most common source of the problem is that the connector cable is not properly plugged in, either at the **monitor** end or the computer end, or that you haven't pushed the "on" button on the monitor itself. If you can hear the monitor humming

On the CD-ROM:
- Website info for printer and modem vendors
- Download up-to-date drivers

but not see anything on the screen, and there's a light glowing to signify that it is switched on, try adjusting the contrast and brightness knobs, usually located under the front face of the monitor. If these steps don't produce a picture, there's probably a fault in the **video card**, or the **monitor** itself, and you'll need to seek tech support.

Invalid system disk

If you turn on your PC and get the message, "Invalid System Disk. Replace the disk then press any key", don't panic – you haven't had **hard drive** failure, you've probably just left a **floppy disk** in the floppy disk drive, which is the A drive of the PC. Due to a legacy from long ago, the PC will start up by first looking to the A drive for its instructions, and because the A drive, i.e., the floppy drive, has a disk in it that contains something other than the start-up instructions for the computer, it will think there's something wrong and just stop, rather than going on and searching elsewhere. Once you take the disk out and press any key on the keyboard, the computer will go searching for its start-up instructions on the C drive, find them, and **boot** up as normal.

Freeze frame

There will be times when, despite your best endeavours and for no particular reason, your computer will **crash** – the screen will seize up, moving the mouse won't move the **cursor** and trying to save your **files** won't work – in other words, your screen has just stopped responding.

Windows hourglass

There's a huge difference between a freeze and your computer taking time to respond, however. If you see the little hourglass symbol in **Windows** or the watch in Mac OS (see both symbols at right), in place of the cursor arrow, you have NOT had a crash – the computer is just taking its time to process your request. Don't click the mouse again, that will just send the computer another instruction to do the same thing, which will confuse it even more. Just wait... check to see if the postman has been, put the kettle on, or fold a couple of towels out of the washing basket, anything that takes a good few minutes. More often than not you'll find your computer has had time to sort itself out, and you can simply continue. You can prevent this happening by giving your computer time to process one instruction before you give it another, so remember to hold off on giving further instructions whenever the cursor turns into an hourglass (PC) or watch symbol (Mac).

Mac OS watch

However, if your cursor *has* disappeared, and you can't save your files or make your computer respond then, sure enough, you've experienced your first crash.

Don't panic. And don't blame yourself, there's probably nothing you could have done about it, and there's probably no damage, apart from the fact that the work you have done between the last time you saved and the moment of the crash will have been lost. Saving your files frequently will minimise the damage and inconvenience you suffer on these occasions.

If your Windows machine crashes

Simply press the Ctrl and Esc keys at the same time; hopefully, that will bring up your Start Menu, and you can simply choose Log Off. Count to 20, then turn the machine on and start again.

If pressing the Ctrl and Esc keys has no effect, hold down the Ctrl and Alt keys, and press the Delete key.

If, during this process, you get a dialogue box that tells you that such-and-such an application is "Not responding" and you are given the option of closing down that application, do it. You will lose any work done since you last saved but there is no way around this; if you can just shut down the application, then you can begin restarting your computer.

If worst comes to worst, and your computer doesn't respond to anything, you'll have to resort to something you shouldn't make a habit of: turn it off at the power switch. Count to 20 before restarting. When it does start up, it will tell you: "Windows did not shut down properly... You may have errors on your hard disk". Don't worry. This message will appear when you restart the computer after you've had a **crash** and had to shut it off, or if you've turned off the computer without shutting it down properly. The computer will start a series of checking procedures using a program called ScanDisk, to ensure all the system components are still in good working order. All you need do is watch and wait – it will place a tick against every category as it checks and establishes a clean bill of health, and when it goes through the list it will then tell you it's now going to start up **Windows**. The procedure will take about two minutes.

To shut down your computer properly

From Windows, you should always follow a series of steps to shut down the computer properly rather than just flicking the switch off. You can use keystrokes or your mouse.

Using your keyboard

Press the Windows key on your keyboard (see picture at right), then select Log Off from the options on the menu that pops up by pressing the letter that's been underlined in the instruction – in this case the letter L in the word Log. This will take you back to the screen which allows you to select your user name, or an option to turn off the computer. Click on that button to turn the computer off. This will bring you to a confirmation screen that gives the options Stand By, Turn Off, Restart. Choose Turn Off to end your computing session.

Windows key

Using your mouse

From Windows, click on the Start Button with the four-coloured flag that appears on the bottom left-hand side of the screen. That will make a menu pop up, then point the mouse at the Log Off option and click once. As with the keystrokes version, you'll step through a series of screens confirming that you actually do want to shut down.

If you get to the final Log Off screen and realise that you don't, in fact, want to log off because you've forgotten to do something, or because a different user wants to do some work, you can choose Restart, or select a different user name, and your computer will go through the booting up process again and you can keep working.

If your iMac crashes

If your iMac freezes up, simply press Option, Apple and Esc together to shut the misbehaving application down. If this doesn't solve the problem, press the Reset button on the right hand side of your computer. You will, of course, have lost any work you did since you last saved, which makes it all the more important to save your work regularly as you go.

Connecting peripherals

The printer connection

To check whether your computer is ready to use the printer you have bought to go with it, click on the Start button on your desktop, then click on Printers and Faxes. If there's a picture of a printer with the name and model of your printer under it, you don't need to do anything. If there's not, choose Add a Printer from the Tasks panel on the left hand side and a **Wizard** will take you through the process of introducing your computer to your printer. If you have a **USB** connection you don't have to go through this process; simply plug your device in and the operating system will recognise the printer type and install the correct driver automatically. Choose exactly the printer name and model number from the lists and click on Next. If the model number is not in the list, you'll need to use the printer company's own driver **disc**, which should be in the box. Put the disc in your **CD-ROM** drive and choose Have Disk instead. Once you have found the right model number and selected it, the computer will load all the information it needs so the two will talk each other's language fluently. Once the process is complete, the Wizard will tell you it is finished and your printer is ready to use.

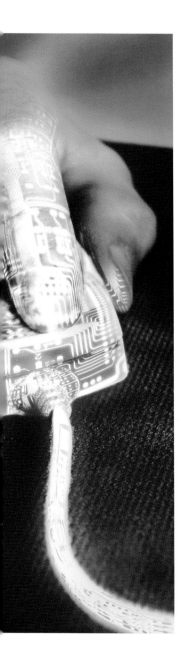

PRINTER PROBLEMS

Often, problems with your printer are simple ones. Check that:

The printer cable is firmly attached to both the computer and printer, that the power cable is plugged in and switched on at the wall, and that the printer itself is switched on.

If the light is on but nothing's happening, check that the paper is loaded properly. If it's not in straight, or not in far enough, often the printer decides the paper tray is empty.

If the printer prints a page but it's all hieroglyphics, you've probably installed the wrong printer driver. Check that the make and model number you select from the list of drivers matches your printer's specifications exactly; choose the right one by selecting it in the Printers box. If you have the right driver, the paper is in straight and it still doesn't work, check that the ink cartridges are properly fitted. Take them out and click them back into place, press the reset button and try again.

If you still have a printer problem, check the progress of the document you are printing: click on Start, and from the right hand panel choose Printers and Faxes. In this window, the left hand task panel will display an option to "See What's Printing". Clicking on this option will show the status of any document either in the printer or in the queue.

If all these steps fail, you will need tech support. When you call, have the model and serial numbers handy.

Connecting a modem

To add a new **modem**, click on the Start button, choose Control Panel then Printers and Other Hardware, then select Phone and Modem Options. Choose the Modems tab and follow the onscreen instructions. If the modem is plugged in, Windows will more than likely detect it, otherwise click Next to select your modem type from a list. Remember to be exact. If your modem type is not on the list (this is extremely unlikely) click Have Disk instead, and load your modem manufacturer's **driver** disk.

If you get the error message "No dial tone detected", check the connection between modem and telephone outlet, and also that the modem is turned on and active, i.e., that the little lights on the front panel are winking. If all the modem's outward vital signs are good, but you continue to get this message, unplug the modem from the telephone outlet and try making a call with a normal telephone – it could be a problem with the line rather than the modem. If a phone can sustain a call but the modem can't, you'll need to call the modem manufacturer for more specific advice.

If the modem tries to dial up and you get the message, "The computer you are dialling into cannot establish a Dial-Up Networking connection. Check your password, and then try again", it's not a modem problem, but something to do with your **ISP** account, password or a connection problem at the other end. Turn the modem off, then on again, and try once more, including re-typing in all the information in your connections box, rather than relying on what's already there, and if you get the same response, call your ISP (Internet Service Provider). Tech support will either tell you what's wrong with your account, or talk you through the problem.

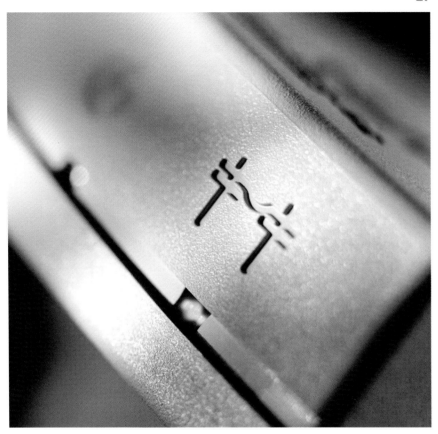

Internal modems are much trickier to troubleshoot, because they don't wink and blink to let you know whether or not they are processing. The suggestions for troubleshooting an external modem are relevant, but if you have to resort to tech support and the technician tells you there's a problem with the modem, it's advisable to take the computer in rather than try and replace the **modem card** yourself.

Shape up your operating system

For 99 per cent of your **software** use, all you'll ever have to do to get it working is push the on button – pretty much everything you'll need to use will have been pre-installed by your retailer or computer manufacturer.

However, most retailers/manufacturers will set up the operating system in a default, and usually impersonal and plain, style. If you're not content with the interface you see when you start up your computer, there are a few simple steps you can take to make it more individual.

But first, a little general information on getting around in the major operating system types, Windows and Mac OS.

Using the mouse

Windows mice have two buttons, Mac mice have only one.

If you have a **Windows** mouse, use the left mouse button to launch applications, select items, and so on. Use the right mouse button to activate other functions, such as making desktop **icons** for your most frequently used applications, as explained further on in this chapter. When an instruction says click, you can assume it means click the *left* mouse button. If you are supposed to click the *right* mouse button it will specify right-click.

You can practice mouse movements playing some of the games and puzzles you'll find included on the **CD-ROM** at the back of this book.

If you have a Mac mouse, you only need one button, because functions that are accessed in Windows by the right mouse button are unnecessary on the Mac – either because the file hierarchy is different, for instance, or because those functions are reached through single or double clicks on pop-up or drop-down windows or dialogue boxes.

DESKTOP THEMES

Windows has a range of desktop themes, usually pre-installed on your **hard drive** or found on one of the operating system CDs that come with your computer. To add a desktop theme – sound, background and a **screensaver** – go to the Start menu, then Control Panel, then Appearance and Themes. Click on the task you're trying to achieve from the list, such as changing your theme. Choose the theme you prefer, and click OK. To load a theme from our own CD-ROM, put the CD into the computer, click the Browse button and make your choice, them click OK.

On the CD-ROM:
- Hone your mouse skills
- Create background and desktop options

Finding your way around Windows

To navigate your way around **Windows**, use the mouse to move your **cursor** around the screen, or any of the keyboard shortcuts found on pages 44 and 45.

Start button

The key to getting around is the Start button, found in the bottom left-hand corner of the screen (pictured at left). The Start button launches the Windows menu, the place where you can find everything you need.

You can launch the Windows menu by taking the cursor to the Start button with your mouse and clicking once, or by hitting the [⊞] key on your keyboard, normally found between the Ctrl and Alt keys on the left side, and next to the other Alt key on the right side of most standard desktop keyboards. If you have an old keyboard that doesn't have a Windows button, to launch the Windows menu without the mouse, hold down the Ctrl key and press Esc.

Rolling the mouse over All Programs will give you a complete list of what's on your hard drive. Further up, the left-hand panel of the window stores all your frequently used applications. Windows will learn by your usage, over time, which applications should be in this panel, and add them for you. Alternatively, you can speed things up for yourself by dragging a document or function there and dropping it in.

Folder icon

The right-hand panel holds the folders for all the other applications and functions your computer has in store. My Computer, for example, offers a list of all the pieces your system is made of, including what's in the system unit, such as hard drive, **CD-ROM** and **floppy drive**, as well as external devices such as a printer, scanner or a digital camera. Clicking on any component, such as the hard drive, brings up a summary in the Details panel on the left-hand side of the screen; this summary contains key information about the component, such as total hard drive capacity, and remaining free space.

To navigate around, use the Back and Forward buttons on the top left-hand side of the screen, or to shut a window down, go to the X on the top right-hand side of the window.

Launching an application in
Windows XP

To launch an application in Windows

Windows XP is set out in terms of tasks, rather than applications, so instead of "launching an application", think "create a document". To start a new document, or open one you've already created, simply click the Start button and choose My Documents. To create a new document, click File, then New. This will launch Microsoft Word. To carry on working in a document you've already created, find the name in the folder, and click on it to launch it. Windows also stores your most recently used documents in a folder called My Recent Documents, so they are easier to retrieve. So if you worked on something yesterday, to find it today, simply look there.

You can also store files of different types, such as music files, or photographs, in folders called things like My Music, or My Pictures rather than prosaic application names, such as My Graphics files, or My Spreadsheets!

32

Creating desktop shortcuts

Setting up desktop shortcuts in Windows

If you plan to use a document or application frequently, and don't want to go through the menu structure to get to it, you can create what's called a desktop shortcut, which is a little icon on the desktop, which will launch your application or document straightaway. For example, if you keep daily track of something, such as rainfall, a diet or a planting schedule, or if you keep your diary on the computer, you might want simpler access to it; just a simple click on a picture on the screen, and you're in. This is where a desktop shortcut comes in handy. To create a shortcut you'll use both right and left mouse buttons. Find the application or document you'd like a desktop shortcut made for, by looking in the Start menu, as before. If it's an application, the name will be in the applications panel, if it's a document it will be inside one of the folders. Click the right mouse button over the application or document name to bring up a menu box. Choose Send To from this menu box by clicking the left mouse button, then Desktop (left mouse button again). This will create a shortcut icon from which you can launch the document directly.

Finding your way around Mac OS 9 and Mac OS X

The Apple menu is the place to go to find your way around Mac OS 9, and can be found in the top left-hand corner of the screen. Click once to drop the menu down, then make your selection from the list. As described in the Windows desktop section, you can find your way around using either the mouse or keyboard shortcuts (page 44).

The keyboard shortcut keys are found next to the menu option, there is a curly symbol and a shortcut letter. That curly symbol is the Command key – you'll find two of them, one each to the immediate left and right of the space bar. Use the Command key the same way you'd use the shift key. In Mac OS X the Apple menu is called the Go menu, but the process is quite similar. Click once on the Go menu to drop the menu down, and make your selection. Applications is a key place on this menu to start looking when you want to change something.

Apple menu

Setting up desktop aliases on your Mac

Making instant access buttons for applications on your Mac desktop is very simple. While in Windows these are called Desktop Shortcuts, in Mac-speak they are called **Aliases**; the principle is much the same. To create an alias of your hard drive if you're using Mac OS 9, click on the hard disk to select it, and it will darken. Go to the File menu and select Make Alias. A second icon immediately appears near the hard disk icon. Its name is in italics and has the word "alias" added at the end. It also has a little curved arrow in the bottom-left corner of the icon. The italics and the arrow signify that the icon is that of an alias, not the real thing. Now double-click on the hard disk to open it. Find the System Folder and double-click to open it, and place the hard disk **alias** you created into the Apple Menu folder you find inside the System folder.

Now click on the Apple Menu on the top left-hand side of the screen, and the alias will have been added to the list that drops down. From now on you can look in your hard disk without having to close or hide windows.

Adobe Acrobat alias

CREATING YOUR OWN DESKTOP THEME IN WINDOWS

The graphic you choose should be in a digital file, unless your computer set-up includes a scanner and you can digitise your own. The file should be any graphics file, either a bitmap (.bmp), a .tif or a JPEG (.jpg) file. The name of the file will thus be bobbybirthday.tif or mycat.jpg, or similar. When you have the file either on disk or in your scanner, save it to a folder you'll remember. Follow the same steps to Customise My Desktop (see page 35, To change your background or desktop theme in Windows XP), but instead of clicking on an established theme, click on Browse, then the folder containing your specified file, then click Apply, then OK. If you find a website graphic that you like, right click on it, then choose Set as Background.

To make the same easy access to a folder, or even a document you plan on working on frequently, you can also make an **alias** of it in the same way, and place it either in the Apple menu or straight on the desktop. You don't even have to really know where it is or what it's called. Go to the File Menu and choose Find, or type ⌘ and F. This launches Sherlock, the Mac OS finder utility, which will find your **file** by name, or the first few letters of it. Type in the name, or part of it, and press Enter. Sherlock is very literal, so be as specific as you can, otherwise you'll get a search result which is too wide, and thus not relevant.

If you see the one you want, however, scroll down with the arrow keys, or roll down with the mouse and click once. The Sherlock window will then show you the path to the document you're looking for. Double click on the folder immediately above it, to open the folder that contains the folder or document you want.

In Mac OS 9 you make an alias of the folder or document in exactly the same way as explained for the **hard drive** – using the Command and M keys or selecting the Make Alias option from the File menu.

To make a desktop alias, click on the name of the folder or document you just made an alias of and drag it onto the screen and release the mouse button.

Changing the name of your alias is also simple. When you first create an alias, the name is "selected" – whatever you type will replace the name. At any time you can change the name of any **icon** by clicking once directly on the icon's name. The text is selected and you can write over the top of it or edit it like word processor text.

To make an alias in Mac OS X is drop dead simple. One of the features of Mac OS X is a Dock, or bar containing applications and functions, which sits either on the side or bottom of your screen. To create an alias, simply select an item from anywhere in Finder, or use Sherlock to find it, and drag it to the dock (by holding the mouse button down over the application name and moving the mouse to the dock, dragging the application icon with it). When you release the mouse button, your alias is automatically created, and waiting for you in the dock.

Customising your desktop

The colour or pattern of your screen is called the background. Both **Windows** and Mac offer a range of pictures and designs to choose from, or you can create your own, or choose one from the selection we've provided on the **CD-ROM**.

To change your background or desktop theme in Windows XP

Click the Start button to pull up the Windows menu and choose Control Panel, then Appearances and Themes. This will launch a window with a number of different tabbed options, for changing the look of your desktop: background, appearance, **screensaver**, settings (such as the number of **pixels** or colours you want your **monitor** to display) and so on. The resolution settings are set at default levels and should be fine for most standard applications use and should only be altered if a particular application (such as a game or graphics package) recommends higher resolution for better performance.

MAKING YOUR OWN BACKGROUND IN MAC OS

Making your own background for your Mac desktop is easy if you have the picture you want to use stored as a graphic file somewhere on your hard drive. Again, it can be a file of any of the commonly used graphics types, .bmp, .tif or .jpg. Follow the same steps, through Appearances (see To change the appearance of your Mac desktop, on page 36), but to find your picture file hold down the Command key and click on the Folders icon. You'll then see the pathway where the folders come from, and you can look through for the name of your picture file, click on it, and it will become your background.

Click on the tab describing the aspect you want to change, to bring that page to the front, and select the colour or pattern you want. The Display box has three options: Centre, Tile and Stretch. Centre will put the chosen pattern only in a little box in the centre of the screen, Tile will extend it to the whole screen and Stretch will magnify the pattern so it looms large out of your monitor at you!

If you have set up a password in the User Accounts section (see facing page) you can also choose to only have the screen saver "wake up" when you type the password. This isn't particularly useful in home situations – except if a nosy neighbour drops in while you're doing the tax return – but is very useful in office situations, where you can be called away from your desk in the middle of important and confidential work.

When you have settled on a pattern, screensaver and appearance that you like, click on Apply, and then OK.

To change the appearance of your Mac desktop

To personalise your Mac desktop, the principle is much the same as in Windows, though the key word is Appearance. Start at the Apple menu and click on Control Panels, then Appearance, then choose the desktop tab. Here you'll find a raft of themes and designs. Simply click on the one you like – it's automatically applied when you click the Set Desktop button.

The process is exactly the same for changing the appearance, the colour of the default highlight, the kind of font used, desktop patterns or for placing a picture on your desktop, either instead of or on top of the new colour or background design you might have chosen. This can be a picture from the gallery on offer as part of the Mac's own library, or one you choose from the CD at the back of this book, or your own choice, either a favourite painting, or a picture of your children, pet or spouse.

If you're using Mac OS X, click on the Apple Menu, then on System Preferences. Then under Personal, click on the Desktop button, and simply follow the directions.

Multiple users

In Windows

Setting up your computer to be used by more than one person enables each family member to have their own personalised desktop and, if appropriate, access to a different set of applications. When one member turns on the computer, they'll be asked to log on with a password. The computer will then **boot** up according to that person's desktop theme, applications shortcuts and so on.

To set your computer up for this, go to the Start menu, then choose Control Panel, then User Accounts to add new accounts (i.e., new user profiles) or to add a password or change details, such as who should have access to specific documents or applications.

In Mac OS

To set up your Mac to be used by more than one person, go to the Multiple Users control panel, click and bring up the panel on the screen. The Owner account, which is really like an administrator's log, has power over all the other accounts.

To add another user, click New User and type in a name and password. You choose a picture, either from those supplied or you can drop in one of your own – such as a photograph of the person, if you have one as a graphics **file** – to identify the user and the account.

The Mac is more creative in this regard than Windows as, instead of a password, you can use a voiceprint to identify yourself. To set up a voiceprint, go to the Set Up Assistant; the system will ask you to choose a phrase and repeat it five times. It will record the wave patterns of your voice each time, then take a median sample of those five wave patterns and allow access only to someone who sounds just like that. Foolproof, and easy as pie for people who have trouble remembering passwords.

If you're using Mac OS X, click on the Apple menu, then select System Preferences. Click on Users (inside the System bar), then New User, and follow the instructions.

TIPS FOR MULTIPLE USERS ON MAC OS

If you're trying to set up a voiceprint, do it in a quiet room, as ambient noise is also recorded, making it hard to achieve an exact voice match.

To put a clamp on what the kids might find trawling through your accounts, or on the **internet**, you can use the Limited User tab in Mac OS 9 to set limits on where they can go on the **hard drive**, or restrict access to applications such as Netscape or Internet Explorer.

Bans or permissions can also be set globally for all users. You can even control use of **CDs** and **DVDs** and, if you have a **floppy drive** (which most iMacs don't), the use of floppies.

Under Mac OS X, every user has a discrete set of applications and documents and cannot interfere with anyone else's unless the document is explicitly marked as a shared document.

Working in applications

Getting used to working in applications of all types is a bit like the old joke: How do you get to Carnegie Hall? Practice, practice, practice.

No 60-second tour in a handbook will ever replace just sitting down at your computer and having a go.

That said, however, here's a quick introduction to a few of the basic functions – and the **icons** associated with them – that will make your life easier.

Along the top of the screen you'll find a row of little pictures, which are shortcuts to certain commonly used functions for creating, printing, saving and closing **files**, for example, or moving text around in a document, or from one document to another, and for changing the way the text looks.

The demarcation between **Windows** and Mac all but disappears at this point, because the major **software** vendors all supply versions of their products for both and, most of the time, these work exactly the same way on both platforms.

Applications icons

To use any of the icons, roll the mouse up so that the **cursor** rests over the picture, or icon. The name of its function will appear so you can check you've got the right one. Then click once to activate that function.

The following icons are common to Microsoft applications, used on a large percentage of the world's computers. Pictures in other applications will look very similar, because the industry at large has finally recognised the benefit of making this computer-learning business as simple for all of us as possible, and decided that what it calls a "common look and feel" was a good start.

COPY THAT

Mastering the shortcuts for copying and pasting will save you lots of time and effort. If you have a particular phrase, such as "not including GST", that recurs frequently throughout a document you're creating, rather than type it over and over, copy it the first time you type it (Ctrl + C), and then insert it, or "paste" it (Ctrl + V), wherever else in the document you want it to appear. The "clipboard" onto which the phrase is pasted only saves the most recently copied or cut text, however, so if you copy or cut something else after "not including GST", your phrase will be overridden.

On the CD-ROM:
■ A printable poster of keyboard shortcuts

Working with documents

 Create a new document

 Open a document
that already exists

 Close the current document

Note: Make sure you **save** your work before you click this button! If you haven't, it ought to prompt you with the message "Do you want to save the changes you made to (document name)?" Always click "Yes" or, if you change your mind and don't want to close it after all, click "Cancel". Choosing "No" will close the document without saving your changes.

 Save the document you're
working on right now

Note: If you want to save a copy of the **file** to a different place, or under a different name, go to the File menu in the top left-hand corner of the screen, click once to drop it down, and choose Save As instead.

 Send an e-mail

Note: You must have an **e-mail** package installed for this **icon** to work. When you click on it, the computer searches to see what information it has about your e-mail set-up and makes an educated guess about how you'd like to send the e-mail, based on the default settings.

 Print a document

 Print preview

This function will show you what your document is going to look like when printed, i.e., how much margin space it has, whether it nearly fits on a single page, etc. Use this function to check and massage your document before you actually print it out, and thus avoid wasting paper.

Working with text in a document

First of all, choose a type-style and size by clicking on the down arrows of the font bars that appear at the top of your screen. Most applications will not only show you a list of fonts available, but will write the name in that type style, so you can see what the text will look like. Click on the type-style you like, and it will become the type-style for that document. To choose a font size, click on the down arrow next to the number bar and select a size from the options available.

To set both the type-style and size as your default, i.e., the size and type you'd like for every document you create (unless you specify otherwise in each new document), click on the Format menu, select Font, and choose the type-style and size you'd like, then click on Default. The software will confirm that that's what you want to do. Simply click on "Yes", and it's done.

The following useful functions are
activated by clicking on these icons:

 Spelling and grammar checker

 Cut text out of its current place

 Copy text (and leave an original in the current place)

 Paste text either cut or copied from previous place

 Make text bold

 Italicise text

 Underline text

 Align text with the left-hand margin of page

 Centre the text

 Align text with the right-hand margin of page

 Align copy so that text meets both left- and right-hand margins

 Find a word or phrase in the text. This is useful if you realise you've used a wrong word or figure and want to change every incidence of it.

To highlight a portion of text, to copy or move it around, take the **cursor** to the beginning of the piece of text you want to move, and hold the mouse button down, and move your mouse until as much of the text as you want is highlighted, then release the mouse button.

Then, take the cursor up to the icons bar and click the  to copy, or the ✂ to cut it out. Now take your mouse to the place you want the text to be inserted (called "pasted"), click once to set the cursor in the right spot, then go back up to the icon bar and click on the .

If you go too far, or highlight too much text, just keep your finger down and go back or, if you want to start again, release your finger, click somewhere else in the text to get rid of the highlight, and start again.

Note, however, that if you press the spacebar or another key while the text is highlighted, your computer will assume you want to replace all that text with the keystroke you've just made, and you'll lose it all.

If you accidentally wipe out a lot of text this way, go straight to the Edit menu at the top of the screen, drop it down and click on Undo Typing. This action will restore your highlighted text. This will only work if you do it straightaway.

If you have highlighted and deleted a portion of text by accident, the same action will restore it, except that the instruction under the Edit menu will read Undo Clear. It's the same function, however.

Adding highlights

To bold text as you go, click the **B** button before you type the text you want in bold, and then click it again when you have finished.

To italicise text as you go, click the *I* button before you type the text you want in italics, and then click it again when you have finished.

To underline text as you go, click the $\mathbf{U}$ button before you type the text you want underlined, and then click it again when you have finished.

To bold, italicise or underline after you have finished typing, simply go back with your cursor to the beginning of the patch of text, click and hold the mouse down to highlight what you want changed, and then click on the appropriate button.

To do the same, but using the keyboard rather than the mouse, Press Ctrl and either B, I or U depending on which effect you're after, and then type the words you want bolded, italicised or underlined, and then Ctrl B, I or U again to finish.

To apply these effects after the fact using the keyboard, go to the beginning of the text you want modified and hold down the Ctrl and Shift buttons and advance a word at a time using the ⟶ key until as much of the text as you want is highlighted, then press Ctrl and the corresponding letter for the effect you want.

For more keyboard shortcuts, see pages 44-45.

Colour and highlight

To highlight text in a document without changing the colour of the actual words, choose the ✏ button or, to make certain words or entire blocks of text stand out by making them a different colour, choose the 🅐 button. Choose from the rainbow of colours available or get creative by clicking on More Colors, then Customize to blend your own hues from the palette.

A TIP FOR MICROSOFT USERS

To bold a single word or a couple of words, without taking your fingers off the keyboard, type an * immediately in front of the word or phrase you want to bold and then another * immediately at the end of it. Microsoft Word will interpret that as an instruction to bold the word, and do it automatically. You have to do it as you go, however – you can't put in asterisks afterwards and expect the software to understand that you want to apply a bold text effect retrospectively.

Keyboard shortcuts

Keyboard shortcuts are ways of getting around the screen and performing functions on your computer using key strokes; such shortcuts are faster than using a mouse.

It's somewhat ironic that keyboard shortcuts can be easier than clicking a mouse, considering that the mouse was invented to make computing simpler; before the advent of the mouse, every input to the computer was via the keyboard.

Nevertheless, learning these keyboard shortcuts for Mac and Windows will save you time and increase your dexterity with the computer, not to mention impress the kids!

Browser shortcuts

The following shortcuts are used in both Internet Explorer and Netscape Communicator.

To **reload** current page: press **Ctrl** and **R**

To **go back** a page: press **Ctrl** and ⬅

To **go forward** a page: press **Ctrl** and ➡

For both Windows and Mac

Applications such as Word and Excel, or **browsers** such as Netscape Communicator and Internet Explorer, govern their own shortcuts, so it's irrelevant whether you're using a Mac or Windows version of the software program – they work the same in both.

The key is the Control (Ctrl) Ctrl button on a Windows machine, and the Command/Apple ⌘ button on a Mac. Hold down the Ctrl Ctrl or Command/Apple ⌘ button, and then press the other relevant key to perform the following functions:

Select all text: press **Ctrl/Command** and **A**. This selects all the text in the document.

Copy highlighted text: press **Ctrl/Command** and **C**. This is useful if you want to copy some text to another place or document. This replaces the mouse clicks Edit, and Copy, or clicking on the 📋 icon.

Cut text: press **Ctrl/Command** and **X**. This allows you to cut text, figures or pictures from one place, and put them in another. This replaces the mouse clicks Edit, and Cut, or clicking on the ✂ icon.

Paste text: press **Ctrl/Command** and **V**. This is used to put the text you've either copied or cut in its new place. This replaces the mouse clicks Edit and Paste, or clicking on the 📋 icon.

Save a document: press **Ctrl/Command** and **S**. Don't forget to save your work often! The first time you save, the computer will prompt you to specify where you want the work saved and what you want to name the document. Any time you save after that, it will save your changes to the same place.

Close a window: press **Ctrl/Command** and **W**. This closes the the document or page you're working on. The computer should prompt you to save the document before it closes, if you haven't already. Always say "Yes".

Extra shortcuts for Mac users

 to move to the next keyboard focus

Page Up to scroll up one full screen

Page Down to scroll down one full screen

Home to move to the top of the scrolling list

End to move to the bottom of the scrolling list

⌘ and **↑** to move up one level in the file hierarchy, i.e., to get to the folder the current document is in.

⌘ and **Q** to quit

⌘ and **O** to open selected folder or volume

⌘ and **A** select all files that can be opened

⌘ and **F** to find a file or folder

⌘ and **N** create a new folder (Mac OS 9)

⌘, **⇧ Shift** and **N** to create a new folder (Mac OS X)

⌘ and **M** create an alias

Extra shortcuts for Windows users

Moving text around in a document

Highlight text: hold down **Ctrl** and **Shift**, then press **←** to advance a word at a time, **→** to go back a word at a time, or the **↑** or **↓** to highlight the text a paragraph at a time.

Delete whole line: press **Alt** and **Backspace**

Delete the word before the cursor: press **Ctrl** and **Backspace**

Delete the word after the cursor: press **Ctrl** and **Delete**

Undo the last edit: press **Ctrl** and **Z**

Redo the last edit: press **Ctrl** and **Y**

Moving between applications

Switch between applications: press **Alt** and **Tab**, until the computer scrolls to the one you want, then release **Alt** key. Your document will come to the front.

Working with applications

Exit an application: press **Alt** and **F4**

Access help: press **F1**

Maximise window: press **Alt** and **Spacebar**, then **X**

Minimise window: press **Alt** and **Spacebar**, then **N**

Bring up Start Menu: press **Ctrl** and **Esc**

Minimise all windows: press **Ctrl** and **Esc**, then **Esc**, then **Alt** and **M**

Using the Windows Start key

Launch Start Menu: press **⊞**

Launch Help Menu: press **⊞** and **F1**

Run a dialogue: press **⊞** and **R**

Find a dialogue: press **⊞** and **F**

Launch Windows Explorer: press **⊞** and **E**

Minimise all windows: press **⊞** and **M**

Undo the above: press **Shift** and **⊞** and **M**

A word of warning

More than a few things can trip you up when you're making your first foray into the world of computers. Two big worries would have to be your computer crashing, resulting in the loss of work, and a virus infecting your computer. Another issue to be wary of is ensuring the legality of your **software**.

Why you should back up data

Backing up data is like going to the dentist every six months, even if you know you have perfectly healthy teeth, or taking out home insurance. You'll need to spend an hour in front of the computer once in a while, saving **files**, labelling **disks** and putting them in a safe place. Afterwards, you'll find yourself thinking: "Phwoar, that was a tedious way to spend time," just as you leave the dentist after a trouble-free appointment thinking of all the other, more pressing things you could have been doing. Backing up is just like insurance – in the best case, you'll never need it, but it's worth paying the premiums just in case.

One day, you may well go to the computer, turn it on, and nothing will happen. Despite your best endeavours, nothing will get it working again. Then, when you take it to a service centre, a technician will say: "Sorry, the hard drive's kaput. There's nothing I can do about it. Hope you've backed up?"

Then, you'll be glad you took the time to make copies of your correspondence, names, addresses, phone numbers, birthday book, greeting card designs, tax records, budget spreadsheets, meeting minutes, newsletter templates and favourite website addresses, and that it's all safely tucked away somewhere on disk or CD.

There are various ways you can **back up** (save files), and the best one for you depends on how much information you have and the size of the files you need to store.

SAVING LISTS
Backing up **Favorites** (or Bookmarks) from your **browser**, or names and addresses from **e-mail** software, is easy and wise. Grab the list (**bookmarks** or addresses) by going into Windows Explorer and clicking on the **Windows** folder, then the Favorites Folder. Copy the folder to your back-up disk. If you're having trouble finding your address book, locate a **file** with the **extension** .wab, thus: click on Start, then Find, then Files or Folders, then type in *.wab. The * tells the computer to look for any .wab extensions. That will find your address book file for you.

On the CD-ROM:
■ Trial versions of back-up, disk management and anti-virus software applications

Backing up Word files

The simplest way, if your **files** are mostly Word documents and you don't create or change much information during the course of a week, is simply to buy a box of **disks** and make copies of all your files. To copy a Word file onto a floppy disk (if you have the document open), simply click File, then Save As, then click the down arrow in the Save In bar and click on 3½ Floppy (A:) when the menu drops down.

If the document is not open at the time, simply launch Windows Explorer from the Start menu, find the document you want to save to disk, click on it once with the right button of your mouse, choose Send To from the menu, then choose 3½ Floppy (A:) from the next menu.

Backing up other files

If, however, you need to back up lots of files every week, and those files are large because they contain images, music or video, backing up to disk is not going to work.

In this case, you need to buy a specific back-up device, either a tape drive, a removable storage drive, such as a Zip drive, or a CD writer.

The cost will vary from $200 to $400, and you should be guided by the volume of your data, the regularity with which you'll need to resave work and the cost of the consumables.

CD writers

A CD writer allows you to write up to 650M of data, or save around 70 minutes of music to a CD. There are two kinds of **discs** on the market for this purpose. First, there's **CD-R**, to which you can write information once; these are cheap. Discs that can be written to more than once are CD-RW, and cost around five times as much. The cost of the discs is probably, over the life of a machine, as important a purchase criterion as the cost of the machine.

If you want to record information onto CD to send it to someone, then the single-use disc is all you'll need; if you're planning on using CDs as a back-up resource, re-using them to overwrite updated data is going to be important – the more expensive discs may prove better value.

Viruses – myths and dangers

Anti-virus software: why you need it

The likelihood of your computer catching a **virus** is like you catching the flu – if you stay at home and never expose yourself to the outside world, the chances are very slight.

Similarly with your computer, it's in exposure to outside influences, such as **floppy disks** from other people, sites you visit on the **internet** and **e-mail** you receive – from strangers and those you know – that the dangers lie.

What is a virus?

A virus is a piece of code or a small program that's designed to interfere with your systems and application software. Viruses are hidden inside, or disguised as, legitimate programs or documents, such as an application or e-mail. Latter-day viruses have one additional development – they are self-populating, i.e., they can use your computer's own information (contacts in your address file) to spread further.

Viruses are executable files; that is, they need to execute (i.e. launch and run) themselves in your system in order to do their damage. So if someone gives you or sends you a file with the **extension** .exe make sure you know what it is before you launch it. Launching .exe files, especially if they have arrived in e-mails and are from a stranger, is asking for trouble. If you do open a document containing a virus, the degree of damage and data destruction depends on what sort of virus it is, not on how long you have it open.

Unfortunately, files with other extensions are not exempt. Viruses called macro viruses can live in spreadsheet or word processing documents, and launch themselves while you're working in the document then spread to all of your other documents with the same extension. The most common cause of infection for this type of virus is using someone else's floppy disk in your computer, or opening a document sent as an e-mail attachment. The anti-virus software industry almost has macro viruses under control, however, so up-to-date anti-virus software on your computer is a good measure of protection if you need to share disks regularly.

WHEN IS A VIRUS NOT A VIRUS?

The proliferation of **e-mail** junk (also known as spam), especially e-mails warning of viruses and exhorting the recipient to forward the message to as many people as possible, are also a form of virus, although not in the normal sense; they won't damage your computer's files. They are an irritation, however, because they clog up the world's computer systems, cause unnecessary panic, and are a distraction to the work of the day. Most of the viruses they warn about, with strange names like "How To Give Your Cat A Colonic", never actually existed; they were just the figment of some prankster's imagination, designed to trick well-meaning people into helping perpetuate the fuss. So if you receive such an e-mail, urging you to send it on, think twice before being caught up in the spam scam.

What damage can a virus cause?

A low-level **virus** might make a document behave strangely, move data around or interfere with certain functions. The virus might not let you save the document, or it might not save to the place you elect or, more frustratingly, it might let you save and close the file, but not be able to open it again.

Many new users assume that weird computer behaviour is somehow their fault. Don't blame yourself – if the computer is acting oddly, it may well have a virus.

More pernicious viruses eat data and opening a document (if the application in which it's created is already infected) can be all you need do to trigger a reaction. So documents you created before you accepted one with a virus in it aren't necessarily safe either.

Virus writers are typically like those who graffiti and damage public places – anti-virus experts say the most common motivations are attention seeking and ego gratification.

Ironically, some of the damage done by viruses stems from the fact that the virus writer may not be a skilled code writer at all; his poorly written code might confuse the computer into making a mistake. The result is damage to the computer's working files or to your own documents, but it's not the sort of damage the virus writer intended.

There are literally thousands of viruses, but the number "in the wild" or released on an unsuspecting world, is small.

The more attention-grabbing virus type is the e-mail virus, such as the high-profile Melissa virus or the I Love You bug. Unlike previous generations of viruses, which only damaged the host computer, this generation uses the address book in the host's e-mail package to populate itself to as many people as possible. The Melissa virus set new world records for infecting millions of computers worldwide within hours.

The I Love You bug introduced non-programmers to the .vbs extension, a **file** written in the programming language Visual Basic. Most computer users have no contact with Visual Basic files because they are hidden in the depths of the computer and not something we need to know about. So if you receive an e-mail attachment with the **extension** .vbs, you'll know it's suspect.

How does anti-virus software work?

Anti-virus software companies work towards neutralising, anticipating and inoculating against viruses; when a new virus does occur, a fix is usually developed within hours.

A good anti-virus software program identifies patches of code (within documents and applications) which have been associated with a virus, then tells you the code is present and the application or document needs to be cleaned or, if the damage is terminal, should not be opened.

Installing an anti-virus software package on your computer when it's first purchased is not sufficient, however, as virus writers are evolving new strains all the time. Your anti-virus software vendor will provide regular updates – on **disc** or **downloadable** from its **website**. You should make sure your software is updated at least every three months.

Check out the trial versions of anti-virus software on the **CD-ROM** at the back of this book.

Copyright: the dangers of "borrowing" software

When you buy a shrink-wrapped box with a **CD-ROM** and an instruction booklet inside, what you are really paying for is one licence for that **software**, and the right to use it yourself.

The CD itself is, after all, merely a way of distributing the software to you – the value is not in the **disc** itself, but in the useful stuff on it.

The copyright, and therefore the ownership of the software, remains with the company or individual who designed and developed it. You've paid for usage rights.

Most software for home users is sold on a single user licence basis, that is, to be installed on one machine only.

If you buy a software product and have a go, and then decide you don't like it or it doesn't do what you thought it would, you can perfectly legally delete it off your system and give it away to a friend. If, on the other hand, you like it a lot and keep on using it, and also pass the disc on to a friend to install on his or her machine, you've just infringed copyright, and broken the implicit agreement between you and the software company.

Shakespeare's Polonius, from *Hamlet*, got it right when he advised his son Laertes to "neither a borrower or a lender be" – though he probably wasn't talking about software.

When you "lend" software to someone, you're infringing the terms of your licence and breaching the implicit trust of the software developer. Not all software comes from multi-national companies with huge marketing budgets; some of the world's most innovative products come from small developers who, like small businesses of any kind, work on tight margins – so every licence counts.

When you "borrow" software, you're leaving yourself, and the work you create in the application, vulnerable, because if you ever need tech support or any help with getting it working or troubleshooting, if you don't have a product reference (identification) number, and can't prove you're entitled to their assistance, you won't get any.

Also, if you like the software you're using illegally, and want to **upgrade** when a newer version comes out, you'll find that not having the discs to trade in will make you ineligible for the upgrade price, so you'll be forced to pay full retail anyway, for the new functionality.

In addition, there's the software police. The Business Software Association is a worldwide association of software companies, large and small, which seeks to protect its collective copyright and prosecute any infringements it finds, whether by companies or individuals.

Passing software around, or wilfully installing more copies than you have legal licences for, is a civil breach of the software licence, and the BSA will institute an action directly against the infringer. It's up to a court to decide the magnitude of the penalty, but fines are frequently hefty, depending on the scale of the infringement, and a jail term is not out of the question.

Actively copying software and reselling it, on the other hand, is a criminal offence, and can carry a jail term as well as substantial fines. There are two ways that you, as an innocent software buyer, can fall victim to this kind of fraud; either when you buy illegal software unknowingly, if it's installed as part of a computer bundle you buy, or when you buy extra applications for too-good-to-be-true prices in a flea market.

In the first instance, make sure the shop you buy your computer from can supply you with the discs for all software installed on the machine, and original documentation, not photocopies, otherwise you might reasonably suspect that it's not legitimate. In the second case, use your commonsense; if the product seems too cheap to be true, it probably is.

You won't go to jail for unwittingly buying these illegal licences, but if you get caught they will be seized and, once again, any work you've created in the applications will be gone as well.

Glossary

Access provider another way of describing the ISP (Internet Service Provider).

Alias on a Mac, a copy of an application, folder or document created to make it easier to access regularly.

Back up making copies of all your files – applications and the documents you create – and storing them somewhere apart from your hard drive, so you have a copy if something happens to your computer.

Beta the final pre-release version of a software package. Beta software is often given to the software company's large customers and business partners, to trial for errors and improvements, before the final version is completed and it is released onto the market.

Bit the smallest unit of data, a bit is a binary digit, i.e., either a one or a zero. Eight bits make a byte, and 1000 bytes make a Kilobyte, and 1,000,000 bytes make a Megabyte. Bits are the building blocks of all computer code.

Bits per second (bps) the rate of transmission of data down a telecommunications medium, typically a telephone line. Measured in Kilobits per second (Kbps), Megabits per second (Mbps) or Gigabits per second (Gbps).

Bookmark a saved link to a web page, so you don't have to retype the web address every time you want to visit it. Also called Favorites.

Boot to boot the computer is to load the operating system into the computer's memory, i.e., get it going. Computers boot up automatically as soon as you turn them on.

Browser the software that helps you navigate your way around the World Wide Web. A browser is a framework that makes going from one web page to another a simple matter of clicking with your mouse on a Hyperlink, or underlined word. Netscape Communicator and Microsoft Internet Explorer are the two best-known browsers.

Burning CDs the process of putting software data onto a CD for distribution.

Byte a unit of data that is eight binary digits (bits) long.

Cache a place that your computer stores information, usually temporarily, for faster subsequent access. In the context of the net, a computer will cache a web page so that, next time you access it, the computer only downloads the elements that have changed, rather than the whole thing, so the page comes up faster. In the context of a computer, disk caching is the way a computer files recently accessed data to make it faster to retrieve, either in a reserved area of RAM or a special reserved place on the hard drive; cache memory is Random Access Memory that the computer can access faster than standard RAM.

CD-ROM (Compact Disc Read Only Memory) an adaptation of the now familiar format for storing and playing music, used for storing and "playing" all kinds of software on your computer. CD-ROMs are recorded digitally, and have quickly replaced floppy disks as a way of storing and distributing computer software of all kinds. All software, unless it too small to warrant the space available on a disc, is distributed on CD-ROM, and accessed by putting the silver disc in the CD-ROM drive (usually the D drive) in your computer. CD-ROMs are written once, and can't be added to or changed by users. They are a convenient way of adding functionality to your computer without clogging up too much hard-dive space, as most of the complex instructions used to run the program are stored on the CD and only accessed by the system when you put the CD in the drive. A CD-ROM has a capacity of up to 600 megabytes of data.

CD-RW (CD Read/Write) blank discs for recording your own files and music, which sometimes can be used more than once.

Chatting "talking" in real time to another person over the net using your keyboard instead of your voice. The computer screen splits into two or more sections, so you can see both or all sides of the conversation.

Chat room specially set up places on the internet for like-minded people to meet and discuss their interests.

Chat software free software which enables two or more people to have an instant conversation on-line in real time using the keyboard rather than their voices.

Chip another word for the microprocessor, the part that drives the computer and determines its capacity and speed.

Clock speed refers to the speed at which your microprocessor works, and is measured in Megahertz (MHz) or, increasingly commonly, in Gigahertz (GHz).

CPU (Central Processing Unit) the main processing component of the computer; soldered to the motherboard, the CPU is housed in the system unit.

Crash your computer will, periodically, and for no logical reason, decide it's confused, overloaded or unable to carry out your instructions. Don't panic – it's probably not your fault. For a PC, press Ctrl, Alt and Delete together, wait for the computer to reboot, and then carry on. For an iMac, press Option, Apple and Esc. The unpredictability factor of a crash is reason enough to save your work frequently as you go, or you could lose it.

Cursor the blinking line on the screen that shows you where you are. To move the cursor, move your mouse to where you want to type and click once.

Cyber prefix used to denote anything connected with the internet, as in Cyberspace, a commonly used word to describe that intangible space covered by the internet and the World Wide Web.

Cybercafe a cafe or coffee shop that has computers installed so you can surf the net. Also called an Internet cafe.

Database a collection of data organised in a structured way so that it is easy to add to, manage and make use of. Databases can be as complex as the bank's records of every customer and their transaction history, or as simple as your name and address book, or Christmas card list.

Desktop computer a computer. The use of the word simply differentiates it from a notebook (laptop) computer or a handheld, such as a Palm.

Digital camera a digital camera writes the elements of the picture it takes digitally rather than storing the image on film. This has the benefit of making pictures easy to transfer from your camera to the hard drive of your computer to use in making your own cards, sending happy snaps in e-mails, or simply storing your pictures in a guaranteed perfect state, either on your hard drive, or saved to a CD-ROM.

Disc as in compact disc. Disc with a "c" because it's circular, not square, like a floppy disk.

Disk drive see Hard Drive.

Disk also known as the floppy disk. Today's PCs include a 3½-inch floppy disk drive. The diskette itself has a capacity of 1.44 Megabytes, which used to be a big deal, but is now chickenfeed. Floppy disks are, however, useful for saving files to transfer from one computer to another. Apple's iMac has done away with such old technology, although users who really want one can buy an external floppy drive as an optional extra.

Document a file created in a word processing application. See also File.

Download describes the process of getting information from the internet to your computer. The reverse process, of posting your own information onto a web page, or sending e-mail, is, quite logically, and conversely, known as uploading.

Drive see Hard Drive.

Driver the small software program that introduces your computer to the various peripheral devices you want to use with it, such as a printer, modem, digital camera, scanner, etc. The driver contains the specific instructions that peripheral device needs to work properly with your system.

DVD (Digital Versatile Disc) the new generation alternative to CD-ROM, an optical disc technology. Its capacity is 4.7 Gigabytes, on one side – enough to store a 133 minute movie, or alternatively sound and data files. It can also store information on both sides in two layers, bringing its capacity to 17 Gigabytes.

E-mail is electronic mail, "letters" you send via the internet.

E-mail address an address comprising your name or part of it, the @ symbol, the company or service provider on whose server the address resides, and some sort of tag such as .com, which signifies the kind of company it is, and sometimes a country signifier such as .au or .nz. You need an e-mail address to send and receive electronic mail, and you can send it to anyone who has an e-mail address.

Expansion slot provides room for you to add extra drives, more memory, or other components to a computer; for example, a DVD as well as a CD-ROM drive, a Zip drive for backing up your files, or an extra hard drive, if you're running out of storage space.

Extensions see File Extensions.

FAQ (Frequently Asked Questions) most web sites will have lists of these as standard pages, as an easy way of getting you up to speed on their particular technology or realm of interest.

Favorites a list on your computer's browser of the places you frequent most on the net. You can activate any site on this list by clicking on the name; there's no need to type in the web address. Also called Bookmarks.

Fax/data/modem card if you choose an internal modem when you purchase your computer, it will probably be one that offers multiple functions, so you can use your computer as a defacto fax machine as well as connecting to the internet.

File/File extensions the common word to describe any piece of work you create and save, whether it's words, numbers, images or sounds. File types are defined by the extension, i.e., the letters after the name of the document and the dot, which tells the computer, and the user, what kind of file it is. For example, [something].doc is a word processed document, [something].jpg is an image file, and [something].xls is a spreadsheet.

Firewire a new high performance serial bus standard developed by Apple Computer, for connecting various devices to your computer. Firewire replaces the existing connector shape and size with a single plug and socket connection for a wide variety of devices. Firewire also has the advantage of offering far faster data transfer rates, of up to 400 Megabits per second.

Flat panel display smart new alternative to the chunky CRT (Cathode Ray Tube) screens associated with the standard computer. Flat panel displays use sophisticated resolution technologies and take up less space on the desk, but are very costly.

Floppy drive/Floppy disk The secondary disk drive in your computer, designed to make adding files and programs, or saving files to transfer to another computer, a simple task. The standard drive, which takes 3½-inch disks on today's computers, inherited the descriptor "floppy" from its predecessor, the 5¼-inch drive, which was, in fact, bendy. The 3½-inch is, however, quite rigid. iMacs have dispensed with the floppy drive, regarding it as obsolescent technology so, if you want the functionality, you'll have to buy an external floppy drive as an optional extra.

Function keys the keys along the top of your keyboard, marked F1 to F12, that provide shortcuts to frequently used functions.

Gigabits per second (Gbps) billions of bits per second, a measurement of bandwidth, or the rate at which information is transmitted on a telecommunications medium, typically a phone line.

Gigabytes (G) billions of bytes, a measurement of storage.

GigaHertz (GHz) billions of Hertz, a measurement of frequency. Used in the context of the clock speed of the microprocessor.

Graphics pictures, illustrations, photographs, drawings, graphs and charts; information that's created visually rather than as text. Sound or moving pictures is referred to as a graphic.

Graphics accelerator card a chipset attached to a video board, a component that a computer program uses to send and refresh images to the computer's screen faster. A graphics accelerator card is an important consideration in PCs that are to be used for playing fast and complex games, or for manipulating and displaying detailed 2D or 3D images.

Handheld computer a term to describe a fully functioning computer, rather than just a day planner or calculator, that is small enough to fit in the palm of your hand, or pocket.

Hard drive the place where all your applications, and the files you create in them, live. Also called the Disk Drive, and on PCs, it's called the C Drive. The C part is a legacy from when computers had no hard drive, but two floppy drives, one of which held the disk that contained the system instructions, the other held the floppy drive that was used to store and save the computer user's own work. These were designated as the A drive and B drive. So, when hard drives became

standard components, they were allocated the next letter of the alphabet and, even though they now represent the computer's main disk drive, convention dictates they are still designated the C drive.

Hardware the physical pieces of your computer – the system unit, monitor, the hard drive and so on. Technically speaking, add-on devices such as printers, scanners and digital cameras are hardware too, but to make the distinction between the intrinsic system components and these devices, they are usually called peripherals.

Hot plug if a device is "hot pluggable" it means you can attach a peripheral device to your computer while the computer is switched on, without risking damage. They will, in most cases, then automatically recognise each other, and work together.

Hotkeys also called shortcut keys. A combination of keystrokes that perform a function faster than using the mouse. See also Function keys.

HTML (Hypertext Markup Language) the language used to create websites and make the process of getting around on the World Wide Web one-click easy. HTML allows users to transfer dynamically between web pages by clicking on hyperlinked words. See also Hypertext.

Hyperlinks the words in a piece of text or a list that are underlined, and in a different colour; these are live doorways

between sites – clicking on the words takes you to a different page or site. To go back to where you were, click the Back button on the left-hand side of your screen.

Hypertext a language designed to make getting around on the web easy.

Icon an image that represents an application (a software program) or a process, such as printing. To launch the application, or perform the function the icon represents, simply use the mouse to click on the icon.

Inkjet printer cost-effective printer technology in which ink from solid blocks is melted and sprayed across the page. Inkjet printers have made colour printing an affordable alternative for home computer users.

Internet the international, interconnected network of computers known as the internet began life in 1969 as ARPANET. It was originally conceived as a way for university computers to share information and make the most of resources. It was also envisaged as the ultimate security ploy by defence organisations; because of its multifaceted, many pathed nature, information could be routed in more than one direction and continue to travel even if part of the system were bombed or infiltrated in case of war.

ISP (Internet Service Provider) the company with whom you sign up for access to the internet.

IT (Information technology) the phrase that describes the world of technology and the internet. IT&T is the same, but includes telecommunications.

JPEG a file type which describes an image that has been compressed to make it more economical to store and send. Pronounced Jay-peg, the acronym stands for Joint Photographic Experts Group, the committee that devised the notion. The file extension for this kind of file is .jpg.

Kilobits per second (Kbps) thousands of bits per second, a measurement of bandwidth, or the rate at which information is transmitted on a telecommunications medium.

Kilobytes (K) thousands of bytes; a storage measurement.

KiloHertz (KHz) thousands of Hertz, a measurement of frequency.

Laptop computer See Notebook.

Laser printer photocopy-quality printing technology in which an image is "drawn" by laser onto a drum and then "burned" onto the page as it passes across the image on the drum. Laser printing is cost effective in black and white but expensive in colour.

LCD (Liquid Crystal Display) a thinner display alternative to Cathode Ray Tube monitors, LCDs are commonly found in notebook computers. LCD works by blocking light rather than emitting it, and uses less power than similar options, such as gas plasma and LED (Light Emitting Diode) displays.

Megabits per second (Mbps) millions of bits per second, a measurement of bandwidth, the rate at which information is transmitted on a telecommunications medium.

Megabytes (M) millions of bytes; a storage measurement.

MegaHertz (MHz) millions of Hertz, a measurement of frequency.

Microprocessor the processor, or computer chip, built for a microcomputer, i.e., a Mac or PC. In the PC world, the predominant suppliers are Intel and AMD; for Macs, it's PowerPC all the way.

Modem the device that connects your computer to the internet, through a phone line. The word is derived from modulate/demodulate, the process it performs on the signals to translate them from digital (the sort your computer reads) to analogue (the sort the phone line reads) and back again at the other end.

Modem card if your computer's modem is internal, it is just a circuit board with the modem components wired onto it which sits inside the system unit. Thus it's referred to as a modem card, rather than an external modem.

Monitor the screen for your computer; also called a display. The prevailing monitor type is Cathode Ray Tube (CRT), but flat screens are becoming more common.

Motherboard the primary circuit board in your computer; houses the main components, or brain bits, of the computer.

MP3 (MPEG Layer 3) this technology is drawn from part of the MPEG defined standard for compressing audio files, and signifies a new file format for storing, downloading and playing music across the internet. MP3 players, about the size of a Walkman, are taking off, because of their portability and a certain cool factor.

Multimedia in computer speak, a very overused and hyped word which means simply combining elements of sound, colour and movement in a given file or program to make it richer and more interesting to watch, or communicate its message better.

Network two or more computers joined together either by cables, or across a wireless network, or, as with the internet, across phone lines or other network cable infrastructure, for the purpose of making it easy for the users of those computers to share information, or common resources, such as a printer.

Notebook a description which demarcates portable from desktop or handheld computers. Also known as a laptop computer.

Password a unique word you decide on as your identifier to get onto the internet, or access other applications and systems. As with a bank PIN, it's important not to let other people know your password.

PC (Personal Computer) also previously known as IBM-compatible computers, now commonly as Wintel machines (because they are, most often, built on a Windows operating system and Intel processor). The term PC differentiates this kind of microcomputer from a Mac, which has a different processor and operating system.

PC card formerly known as a PCMCIA card, these credit card-sized input/output (I/O) or memory devices are used in notebook computers to easily add extra functionality.

Peripherals external components, such as a printer, scanner, or digital camera which are not intrinsic to your computer.

Piracy using software for which you have no licence. Deliberately copying software either to give away or to sell.

Pixel a contraction of the words picture and elements, pixels are a measure of the dots per inch, or resolution, on your computer's screen.

Platform the type of microprocessor on which the computer is based, and which defines what operating system it needs, thus, PC platform, or Mac platform.

Processor the chip that drives your computer. The speed at which a computer operates is determined by how powerful and fast the processor is. The lion's share of the world's PCs are powered by Intel processors, while Macs run on PowerPC processors.

QWERTY describes the standard keyboard layout; the top six letters, starting on the left, are Q,W,E,R,T and Y.

RAM (Random Access Memory) the easy-to-access place in your computer that stores applications and data while the computer is running, to make response times as fast as possible. RAM is much faster to write to and read from than the hard drive, floppy drive and CD-ROMs, but data is only stored there while your current computing session lasts, i.e., until you turn it off. RAM is stored in small chips in your computer's CPU. Because of the mathematical construct of a computer you need to have matching RAM modules, so you can't have, for example, a 32M chip in one slot and a 4M chip in the other; they have to be the same.

Refresh rate the number of times per second the information on your screen is renewed. The refresh rate depends on the video card your computer uses. Measured in Hertz, a refresh rate of 60 Hertz means your computer's display is refreshed 60 times per second.

ROM (Read Only Memory) unlike data stored in RAM, the computer remembers data held in ROM between sessions, even when the computer is switched off. As the name suggests, ROM contains information that can be read, but not written to. The best example of ROM is the instructions your computer uses to boot up when you switch it on.

Save the process of writing the work you're creating to the hard drive. Saving your work regularly is a good idea, in case of computer malfunction.

Scan/Scanner the process of taking a digital print of an image on paper or other non-digital format, or the device used for this purpose. A scanner can import the image into your document.

Screen see Monitor.

Screensaver a lighthearted animated program that starts up when the computer detects a period of inactivity. Originally designed to stop screen burn, from the same image being left on the screen for an indefinite period, newer screen technology means that today's screensavers are redundant and thus mostly just for fun – a way of personalising your desktop.

Search engine an internet-based piece of software that will take a request for information, go out and crawl the web looking for words that match the request, decide which ones best suit the criteria and build a list of the sites which might fit the search word.

Serial the connection to your computer, or the cable type most commonly used for connecting devices such as a keyboard or a mouse to your computer. Serial connections allow instructions to travel serially, i.e., in sequence, one at a time. Serial ports and connections are being rapidly replaced by USB (Universal Serial Bus).

Shareware software packages that are freely available, usually by download over the internet, on a try-before-you-buy basis. Most developers of shareware are not commercial operators, but people who write software because they have a passion for it. These developers trust the honesty of the person downloading their software to send a cheque if they intend to keep on using the product. Freeware follows the same concept, but the developer simply offers the product and expects no payment.

Site see Website.

Software the programs your computer uses to run itself and perform the various functions you want it to. Software can be loosely divided into two kinds: systems software, i.e., the software, including the operating system, which runs the computer and makes it perform general functions, and applications software, the more specific programs for writing, drawing, making music, calculating and using the internet.

Stuffit a file compression program commonly used on a Mac, for reducing the file size of some work you have created, for the purpose of storing or sending it.

Suite a package of applications offering a range of functions in the one box, e.g., word processing, spreadsheet, e-mail and browser, built to work well together, by using the same commands to achieve similar functions.

Surfing a general term to describe the process of getting around the internet. Usually describes an ambling, exploratory use of the net rather than a deliberate and focused search.

System unit the box (or piece of hardware) that sits on or under your desk; home to the motherboard, disk drives and all the other engine and brain bits of the computer.

TCP/IP (Transmission Control Protocol/Internet Protocol) the basic language of the internet. This protocol, or series of instructions, assembles all the messages and instructions sent across the internet into manageable-sized packets and designs the route for them to take from the departure point to the destination. Because of the multi-pathed nature of the internet, not all of the packets necessarily take the same route or arrive in the same order, they need to reassemble in order to make sense at the destination. TCP/IP takes care of both levels of organisation.

TFT (Thin Film Transistor) a liquid crystal display technology most commonly used in notebook computers. TFT uses a transistor for every pixel in the display, which makes the screen response time (i.e., pixel illumination) much faster. Also sometimes called Active Matrix display.

Twisted pair the ordinary copper wire that connects the phone line to your home. Twisting two wires around each other helps reduce electromagnetic induction. In today's telephone infrastructure, often two twisted pairs are installed in the same cable, which allows homes to use the second pair for a second, dedicated line for a modem.

Typeface a design for a set of characters: letters, numbers and symbols. In computers the typeface is recognised by both the computer and the printer it is to be printed out on, and comes in a range of variations of sizes and styles, such as italic and bold.

Upgrade when the company that developed a piece of software you're currently using releases a new and improved version, you can upgrade by overlaying the new parts onto the version you're currently using and deleting the old components, rather than having to reinstall the entire piece of software. Software vendors offer upgrades at far lower prices than full versions of the same product. Upgrades are delivered either physically, on compact disc, or are downloadable from the company's website.

UPS (Uninterruptible Power Supply) an optional device that allows your computer to keep running for a short time – i.e., long enough for you to save any work – even after the main power supply has been lost. A UPS device houses a battery that kicks in as soon as it detects loss of mains power, giving you long enough to save data. It is also useful because it kicks in when it detects a power surge, to protect your computer from any ill effects.

URL (Uniform Resource Locator) the unique address of every website or other resource on the net. A URL for a website on the World Wide Web looks like this: http://www.acpbooks.com.au. Like a street address but in reverse, every part of the address narrows the location down further.

USB (Universal Serial Bus) a Plug and Play standard for connecting devices such as a mouse, joystick or printer to your computer without an adaptor card or the need to turn the computer off to plug the device in. It is fast replacing standard serial and parallel interfaces for these devices.

Video card a secondary integrated circuit board which houses the information to feed information from the brain of the computer to the monitor. The power of the video card (also known as a video board or video adaptor) governs the refresh rate of the monitor, an important consideration if the computer is used for lots of process-intensive graphics or high-speed games.

Virtual in computer speak, the word can be used to describe either the virtual (as opposed to physical) world of the internet, or the computer's use of resources to create pretend storage space out of memory, as in Virtual Memory.

A computer creates virtual memory, and swaps the files between active memory (such as RAM) and other storage devices such as the hard disk, so that it can process, store, recall and then file information faster than it could do if it had to go back to the storage device every time it wanted to use or reuse an instruction.

Virus a program designed with malicious intent, to be installed surreptitiously and do damage to your computer. The most common ways of contracting a virus are sharing floppy disks with someone whose computer has a virus, or in e-mail across the internet. The most notorious e-mail viruses of recent times include Melissa and the I Love You virus. Maintaining up-to-date anti-virus software on your computer is a good start to protecting your data.

Virus control software another way of describing anti-virus software.

Voice recognition software that allows you to speak commands or dictate documents to your computer instead of using the keyboard and mouse. Voice recognition software requires lots of RAM to function adequately.

Web a contraction of World Wide Web (WWW).

Website a place created by companies or individuals to communicate their message or sell their product on the World Wide Web. A website differentiates itself from a web "page" by its complexity and number of extensions.

Windows the prevailing PC operating system, developed by Microsoft, the world's most powerful software company. There are different versions of Windows for various purposes. Your home computer will probably be installed with Windows XP. Other flavours of Windows include Windows 95, Windows 98, Windows 2000, Windows ME and Windows NT.

Wintel a contraction of two of the core technologies which together make up the lion's share of today's PCs – Windows, the operating system, and Intel, the supplier of the microprocessor. A computer might be called a Wintel machine to differentiate it from an iMac, for example.

Wizard The term used in Windows to describe an automated set of instructions for common processes, such as installing new hardware drivers. In Mac OS it's called SetUp Assistant.

Word processor software application for creating letters and documents, featuring a range of fancy fonts, grammar- and spell-checking capabilities and, increasingly, advanced features such as layout options and even web page creation tools.

WWW (World Wide Web) the infrastructure defined by Tim Berners Lee in 1990 to make getting around the internet easier. The metaphor is that of a spider's web, in which everything is interconnected and every place can be reached by many routes.

Index

Editor Julie Collard
Designer Alison Windmill
Illustrator Andrew Joyner
Photography Getty Images
Cover photography Sarah Callister

ACP BOOKS STAFF
Editorial director Susan Tomnay
Creative director Hieu Nguyen
Publishing manager (sales)
Jennifer McDonald
Publishing manager (rights & new projects)
Jane Hazell

Production manager Carol Currie
Business manager Sally Lees

Chief executive officer John Alexander
Group publisher Jill Baker
Publisher Sue Wannan

Produced by ACP Books, Sydney.

Colour separations by
ACP Colour Graphics Pty Ltd, Sydney.
Printing by Dai Nippon Printing, Hong Kong.

Published by ACP Publishing Pty Limited,
54 Park St, Sydney; GPO Box 4088, Sydney,
NSW 1028. Ph: (02) 9282 8618
Fax: (02) 9267 9438.

acpbooks@acp.com.au
www.acpbooks.com.au

Australia Distributed by Network Services,
GPO Box 4088, Sydney, NSW 1028.
Ph: (02) 9282 8777. Fax: (02) 9264 3278.

United Kingdom Distributed by Australian
Consolidated Press (UK), Moulton Park
Business Centre, Red House Road,
Moulton Park, Northampton, NN3 6AQ.
Ph: (01604) 497 531. Fax: (01604) 497 533.
acpukltd@aol.com

Canada Distributed by
Whitecap Books Ltd, 351 Lynn Ave,
North Vancouver, BC, V7J 2C4.
Ph: (604) 980 9852.

New Zealand Distributed by
Netlink Distribution Company, Level 4,
23 Hargreaves St, College Hill, Auckland 1.
Ph: (9) 302 7616.

South Africa Distributed by PSD Promotions
(Pty) Ltd, PO Box 1175, Isando 1600, SA.
Ph: (011) 392 6065.

Dancer, Helen.
Getting started.

Includes index.
ISBN 1 86396 265 4

1. Computers. 2. Microcomputers.
I. Title. (Series: Australian Women's Weekly
Home Library). (Series: Computer basics).
004.16

© ACP Publishing Pty Limited 2002
ABN 18 053 273 546

FAQs (Frequently Asked Questions)

How can I view the CD?

The CD attached to this book runs in a similar way to a website. To view the content, you need a web browser. Common browsers include Microsoft Internet Explorer (IE) and Netscape Communicator. Internet Explorer is pre-installed on all new computers.

What should I do if I don't have a web browser installed?

Don't worry, there are browsers for Windows and Mac available on the CD. For instructions on how to install one, read the file browser.txt located in the root directory of the CD.

Do I need to connect to the internet to use the CD?

No, you do not have to be on the internet to view the contents of the CD and install the software found on the CD. Everything is included on the CD.

Can the CD run on my system?

The CD runs on any machine running Windows 95, Windows 98, Windows ME, Windows XP, Mac OS 9 and Mac OS X. Individual programs and demos on the disc have their own system requirements, which may be higher.

How do I get started?

WINDOWS USERS: Place this CD into the CD-ROM drive and the home page will open up automatically. **NB:** If the CD does not start after 30 seconds, double-click My Computer on your desktop, then the CD icon and then Default.

MAC USERS: Load the CD then double-click on the CD icon that appears on screen, to launch the contents list. Click on Default to open the home page.

How do I use the CD?

Once the home page appears, click on the link "How to use the CDs" for a quick tutorial. Also see "What's on the CDs".

What do I do if I have a problem?

We are happy to provide written technical support for using the CD, but are unable to provide telephone support, or any support for the third-party software on the disc. If you have questions about the CD, contact us via e-mail at acpbooks@acp.com.au or send mail to ACP Books, GPO Box 4088, Sydney, NSW 1028. Alternatively, you can fax us on (02) 9267 9438. Please include details of the problem and a return address, e-mail address (if available) and daytime telephone number so that we can contact you. If your CD is faulty, please contact us for a replacement on (02) 9282 8618. For further help and the latest information, please read the file ReadMe.txt located in the root directory of the CD.